16 GIFTS FROM A STEPMOM

ENCOURAGEMENT FOR THE BLENDED FAMILY JOURNEY

SHARILEE SWAITY

SHARILEE SWAITY

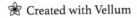 Created with Vellum

To my stepsons

ACKNOWLEDGMENTS

Thank you to the LORD Jesus Christ, without whom I can do nothing. You give me hope to keep living each day and provide all of my needs.

Thank you to my editor, Debra L. Butterfield. I so much appreciate your fierce commitment to detail and high standards. You have shaped my manuscript into something so much better than I ever could have on my own. Thank you for being my coach and cheerleader in this whole process.

Thank you to all the stepmoms who took the time to answer my surveys and do the interviews. You have helped me understand your lives better, so that I can help others in the journey. I appreciated your candour and openness so much.

Thank you to my husband, Vern, who has been patient as I stay up late to write, sometimes (*okay, often!*) leaving other duties undone in my quest to get my words to paper. You were the one who first whispered in my ear ten years ago, "Why don't you write," helping me to resurrect a childhood dream and to never give up.

Thank you to my mom, Sharon Ramona Clark, who taught me how to love unconditionally and never give up on people. You loved writing, too, and shared your passion for pen and paper by example. Some of my greatest memories were when you woke us with a poem you had worked on the night before. I miss you, Mom, and think about you every day.

CONTENTS

INTRODUCTION

Are you a stepmom? Do you feel like your situation couldn't get any crazier? Do you feel like no one could possibly understand what you are going through?

Although you may feel alone in your struggles, the reality is that you are far from alone. One out of every three couples getting married today is forming a stepfamily! [1]

You're part of a growing tribe of women who *step in* to love their partner's kids. You entered the family as an outsider to a pre-existing system with its own customs, traditions and history.

You hope you're making a difference but find the obstacles and rejection overwhelming. You may even secretly wonder if you've made a mistake and fantasize of escaping your situation.

I'm a stepmother, too. My kids are grown now, but I remember well how, at the beginning, I felt invisible, awkward, and even apologetic for invading everyone's space. I wasn't sure of how to connect with the family and felt alone.

I hope this book encourages you and gives you a new vision for your role as a stepmother. You are an unsung hero who has stepped in to love someone else's kids. You were brave enough to take on children who were still hurting.

You have been a stranger in a foreign land, all for the sake of love, for the sake of a new beginning. You are willing to bear the stigma of the stepmother role, to be misunderstood by the world, for the sake of building a new family.

I think the hardest thing about being a stepmom is that you *are* a stranger. It is hard to figure how to build connections with these children that you did not birth, but who are now a permanent part of your life. How do you get to know them and let them get to know you? How do you make the journey to becoming *less* of a stranger?

THE SIXTEEN GIFTS

The sixteen gifts are ways of helping you connect with the kids — endowments that will help build trust and love. They are *gifts* because they are given freely, without cost to the recipient. They often require sacrifice on the giver's part, and like physical gifts, they help to build connections between the giver and the receiver.

Before our marriage, I spoke to my husband's ex-partner and

asked if she was okay with me being in the children's lives. She said yes, and said she'd told her sons another person in their lives meant another person to give them presents.

They were young, and she was helping them see the good side of a confusing situation, but there was an even deeper meaning to her words. We stepmoms have presents to give and not just birthday presents! We provide presents like our unconditional acceptance, our time, and our encouragement.

Each chapter of this book is devoted to a "gift" that stepmoms can offer their family. For some sections, I am sure you will feel a sense of recognition that you are already doing these things. For these chapters, take the time to celebrate your contributions. Other chapters may be new to you and may challenge you to try something new.

The gifts may seem to repeat sometimes or run into each other. For example, patience is part of compassion, and listening is part of encouragement. Think of the gift analogy as a lens that can help us see things in a new way, but the chapters do bleed into one another.

ABOUT THIS BOOK

My book is based on a combination of research and personal experience. I share bits and pieces of my own story. I also conducted several surveys with other stepmoms. Please note that some of the names and details of the stories in this book have been changed to protect anonymity.

In addition, I've spent hours and hours researching academic studies, articles and journals to better understand this complex topic. In my research, I've learned some interesting things that I am privileged to share with you.

Most of all, my desire is that this book will inspire and encourage you as a stepmom. The book is not meant to be a step-by-step manual of blended family living. If that is what you are looking for, I highly recommend the following resource by Jeanette Lofas, founder of the *Stepfamily Foundation*:

Stepparenting: Everything You Need to Know to Make it Work[2]

I hope that by reading my book, you will feel less alone in your journey. I hope these gifts will inspire you to not give up on forming lifetime connections with these children who are now a permanent part of your life!

THE SECRET MILLIONAIRE

To finish off the chapter, I want to share one little story. A few years ago, my husband and I loved to watch a show called *Secret Millionaire.*[3]

Each week, a wealthy businessperson was featured. This entrepreneur had decided to give away a substantial sum of cash. To help him determine where to donate, the future benefactor would disguise himself with a bad haircut and geeky glasses, and volunteer anonymously at several organizations.

After spending a few days at each place, he would choose the most deserving charity and reveal his true identity to them. Being a stepmother is a lot like being a secret millionaire. You've got so much to give to your stepchildren, but it is very likely that they just don't realize it yet.

HOW I BECAME A STEPMOM

I am a stepmom, too, just like you. My step kids are older now but I will always be in their lives. I've been a bonus mom for over ten years now and have watched the boys grow from awkward teenagers to confident men.

In this chapter, I will share how I became a stepmother. You may relate to my story or you may wonder how I could have been so naive. Just know that I write from experience, not just theory. Much of my expertise comes from making mistakes and learning from them. I did not start off as a blended family expert. Let me start at the beginning.

It was 2006. Facebook was barely a thought, and most of us texted via MSN Messenger. Cruising the World Wide Web usually involved a very ugly sound called "dialup." I had gone to a tiny village in Northern Canada to teach high school English. The town was eight hours from the nearest city, the epitome of isolation.

I truly loved it up there in that little town beside the big river. My evening walks were refreshing, and I was mesmerized by the northern lights seen often in the night sky. I loved that I could walk fifteen minutes to my classroom and five minutes to the Northern store the other way.

It was beautiful but also very lonely. After a year in this remote setting, far from everyone and everything familiar, I cautiously dipped my toe into the world of online dating, hopeful but trepidatious. Still full of fear from my last experience with romance, I would barely actually talk to potential contacts.

SINGLE DAD WITH TWO BOYS

One night, however, a profile caught my eye. He seemed to meet my basic requirements. Christian? Check! Gainfully employed? Check! Not creepy looking? Check! You may laugh, but the creepiness factor is a real thing when dating online.

The fact that he lived two provinces away only made him safer: what were the chances that we would actually meet? The title on his description fascinated me. It said, "single dad with two boys."

I'd never considered dating someone with children before, but thought why not? After all, I was a teacher; I was used to dealing with kids. I was pretty sure I would make an awesome stepmom.

All I knew about blended families at that time was from watching *The Brady Bunch*. I can honestly say I had no idea what I was getting into. At 38 years old, I still wanted kids, but my time was running out. Maybe this would be a different path to becoming a mom.

So, I sent a little "wink." He winked back. We wrote messenger chats, which turned into emails, which turned into phone calls. One evening, we didn't want to let each other go and talked all night. He listened intently when I spoke, so different from any other man I had ever known. I felt safe with him; he seemed so loving and kind.

After about a month of frequent communication, Vern asked if I would consider moving closer to him. We had not met yet but felt a strong connection. He told me that he would have considered moving to where I was but would not be able to leave his kids. Although it was very soon, I jumped in and made the decision to move over 1000 miles away, to be closer, and give the relationship a chance. I gave notice to my job and started making plans.

He came to meet me and helped me move across three provinces with a trailer full of furniture, books and papers. Two days after arriving in the city, I met his two boys, aged 10 and 12, and thought they were amazing. I loved being a future stepmom!

Dad was an every-second-weekend parent, and we immediately went about the business of getting acquainted. I learned to play Mario Party (very badly, but I tried!) The four of us went for frequent ice cream walks and playground runs. Every second Thursday was dinner at MacDonald's.

A few months into the relationship, my future husband and I

started to argue more and more until the pressures built, and we ended the relationship.

One of the hardest things about breaking up was losing touch with the boys I had come to love, but it was apparent their dad and I were not ready to be together. We had moved way too fast. After a six-month break, with plenty of reflection time, we decided to give our relationship another chance.

Studies show that many couples entering into stepfamilies make similar choices to ours. They get serious quickly, and then the relationship tends to explode. Some get married early, and others choose to cohabitate. Either way, they are not prepared to deal with the complications and have troubles.

WE WERE OFFICIALLY A BLENDED FAMILY

Vern proposed to me three months later after reuniting, and by March, we were officially a blended family! We included the boys in our ceremony and were excited to begin our new life together.

During our courtship, we had been so focused on figuring out *our* relationship that the details of how we would all live together were overlooked. We took it for granted that things would work out, and I can recall only one or two conversations about how we would function as a family unit.

After the wedding, I loved getting closer to the boys, but it was awkward, too. None of us knew how to relate to each other in this new family dynamic. We had a *lot* of hard years.

I found out later that our problems were typical stepfamily difficulties. We had custody changes and lawyers were involved. It got ugly at times, and there were so many misunderstandings. I freely admit that we made a lot of mistakes. Sometimes, I questioned my reason for being there, but I never doubted that I loved them all.

We did not give up, though, and eventually, things got better. As the boys grew into adulthood, everyone started to grow more comfortable with each other. I knew that we must not have been the only ones who had been through the things we had.

Those tough years are the reason that I've been spending my time creating materials to help those in blended families. I have a passion for helping people who are hurting. I want to provide hope by helping stepmoms see that things will not always be as they are now, and that their struggles are perfectly normal for the situation they are in.

This book is my gift to stepmoms like me who had no idea what they were getting into but are determined to make it work. These sixteen gifts will help you connect with the kids who are now a permanent part of your life.

2

THE STEPCHILD'S LOSS

*H*ow much time have you spent considering what the children in your blended family have been through? It may be uncomfortable to look at, but it is important for truly understanding the kids in your life.

In this chapter, we will reflect on the experience of divorce or bereavement from a child's perspective. Then, we will consider what it is like for a young person to have her father get together with someone other than her mother.

As I write this, a hurricane named Dorian is hitting the coast of the Bahamas, destroying thousands of homes and businesses. Locals are holed up in hotels usually reserved for tourists. People in nearby Florida are waiting helplessly, wondering if they are next.

When these events happen, the entire world gathers around for a while. Television crews rush to the scene; armies and police squads secure safety. The rest of us wonder how we can help. Pleas for donations go out and Go Fund Me pages are quickly assembled.

At first, we are overwhelmed, but after a while, we are no longer as shocked by the constant news of trauma. We may even become jaded and stop taking an interest in what is happening. For the people involved, however, these tragedies are not 10-minute segments on the media screen. Natural disasters will take months to clean up and years to fully recover from.

THE STEPCHILD'S DISASTER

Have you ever stopped to consider that our stepchildren have undergone a form of natural disaster, too? Most have lost the family that they once knew. Whether through divorce, death or breakup, their lives have been irrevocably altered.

Like the ruins of an earthquake, it will take years to rebuild, but you can be a key player in the process. You will not be the stranger on the street clucking sympathetically about a sad story, though. Instead, you will be the volunteer worker who comes in and helps for a lifetime to rebuild that child's life.

This chapter will examine the losses of a stepchild so we can better understand the disasters they have been through. Whether the family has experienced a divorce, a bereavement or a breakup, the family has been through a loss. Children will need to grieve the destruction of their family that they once knew.

THE LOSS OF DIVORCE OR BREAKUP

If you have been seen the popular Netflix series *The Crown*, you will have seen the true story of a king who lost his throne for daring to marry a divorced woman. In 1931, King Edward VIII fell in love with the divorcee, Wallis Simpson, but when the British monarchy refused to allow them to marry, he chose to abdicate his rulership as king and was forced to leave the country in shame.[1]

The incident caused a great uproar. Divorce has always been with us, but today it is much more commonplace and considered much less scandalous. Although it is difficult to measure the divorce rate accurately, one researcher estimates that approximately four out of every ten marriages today will end in divorce.[2]

Another important demographic shift to consider is that living together is much more common than it used to be, meaning that those of the millennial generation are less likely to get married in the first place. Approximately 10 percent of stepfamilies are formed when never-married partners form a relationship with someone else.[3]

In this case, the effects of the breakup are very similar to divorce but without as many legal issues involved. If the split happened before the child was born, the child has never experienced his parents living together, but can still feel the loss of an absent father.

Let's examine all that a child loses when his parents break up. First, the child loses the family that he once knew, and no longer has full-time access to both his mother and father. In the majority of cases (five out of six), it is the mother who maintains custody, so the child has far less time with his father.

The fact that his parents no longer live together means that he cannot go and see either parent whenever he wants, like before, but instead his time is dictated by whose custody he is in at that particular time. The loss of time spent together that occurs after a divorce or breakup should not be underestimated. Time lost together is the biggest loss of a divorce or breakup.

Another important loss is the absolute and utter disruption a child experiences when his mom and dad split up. His whole world is completely turned upside down. Divorce brings unwanted change that is completely beyond the control of a child.

The child is now forced to live in two homes instead of one. For anyone who ever stayed at a cottage, or even gone camping, knows, trying to live in two places is more complicated. You have to remember to pack any belongings you might need for your stay at the other home, and you are continually adjusting.

Going from home to home means getting used to different expectations and rules at each house. Traditions and rituals that Mom and Dad used to do together usually die out. The relationships with their extended families often change, too, as grandmas and aunties struggle to know how they fit into this new complicated family dynamic.[4]

The prevalence of divorce does not translate into making any of these new realities easier for kids. When kids are hurting, they often don't have the language to express themselves, so their pain can manifest in a variety of ways, including acting out, decreased concentration, and poorer academic performance.

Besides the logistical changes that children undergo, there is also the conflict that often accompanies a parental breakup. Watching their parents fight makes them feel helpless and sad. Individuals involved in a divorce usually end up in court proceedings. Studies show that children are often confused by what is happening at court and assume the worst. Studies also show that older children are more likely to feel anger at one or both of the parents going through a divorce. [5]

Many divorced parents are less emotionally available for their children, making it even more challenging for the kids to adjust. Studies show that kids from divorced families are more likely to divorce when they grow up. Researchers have found daughters are affected the worst, with their parent's breakup making them less confident in themselves and their ability to make a relationship work.[6]

THE LOSS OF BEREAVEMENT

Some stepfamilies are formed not from divorce or breakup but rather from the death of one of the parents. If you are a stepmother to a child whose mother has passed, you are entering a very different situation. You will play a different role than the one where the mother is still alive.

When a child's mother passes away, they lose the person they are tied to more than any other. For a child to lose a parent is intensely sad and scary. Children do not get over such a significant loss easily. One research study described it as "a profound psychological insult."[7]

I lost my mother at the age of 29, and the loss was unlike anything I've ever experienced. Those of us who mourn a mother lose a part of who we are; mothers are our very tie to this earth.

Studies have found that many kids are still actively grieving one year later. Two years after the death, many kids experience low self-esteem. Long term, teen girls whose mothers have died are more likely to become teenage moms. Adolescents who have lost a parent are more likely to experiment with illegal drugs.[8]

THE LOSS OF REMARRIAGE OR COHABITATION

Have you ever considered that the wedding that carries such positive memories for you may have had a very different meaning for your stepson or daughter? On your wedding day, he watched his father marry someone other than his mother, officially ending the family he once knew.

In the hilarious campy film *The Parent Trap*,[9] twins plot to get their mom and dad back together. Studies show that many young school-aged children secretly wish their mommy and daddy would reconcile.[10]

Remarriage or cohabitation also means the kids will be spending more time with their stepmother. It is one thing to meet the woman in their father's life through a series of outings, but it entirely another matter to have her living there every single day! Whether the father has full or part-time custody, this will be a big adjustment for all involved.

Children must also now adjust to someone else's expectations. In homes with two sets of children, adjustments are even more complex, with newly formed stepbrother and sister relationships. Another important factor is that stepchildren also lose the unfettered access to their father they enjoyed before you came into the picture.

In conclusion, I hope this chapter has helped you better understand what your bonus child may have been through. Being a stepmom is very challenging, but so is being a stepchild. Understanding doesn't make the difficulties go away, but it puts things into context. Now, let's get to the sixteen gifts that a stepmother can offer to her stepchildren in order to build connection and trust!

3

THE GIFT OF COMPASSION

*H*ave you ever noticed that tragic events seem to bring out the best in people, making them feel compassionate and eager to help? For example, this year, there was a devastating accident with some hockey players in my country of Canada. The whole country seemed to go into mourning.

I think it hit us so hard because hockey is the national passion in our nation. The social hub of most small towns is the arena. Evenings and weekends, cold moms and dads sip on lukewarm coffee, cheering on their jersey-clad munchkins.

On April 6, 2018, a junior team from Humboldt, Saskatchewan, were on their way to a playoff game two hours away. Players and coaches were packed together in a stinky bus, getting ready to battle their opponents. Seemingly, out of nowhere, a semi-truck appeared and crashed into the side of their vehicle. Fourteen individuals lost their lives on impact. Three more lost their lives soon after.[1]

Almost everyone in Canada has a hockey player in their circles. Losing these promising players, along with their coaches, felt like losing one of our own. The feeling of compassion was instinctual and automatic.

When tragedies occur, it seems natural to put aside our pettiness. We are caught up in the feeling that we are all human beings, vulnerable and fragile. We see past the insignificant and realize how close we are to each other.

When someone loses a spouse, or a marriage, or a parent, the tragedy is private but just as devastating to the one involved. When we truly understand the losses of our stepchild, we can't help but feel compassion.

Compassion allows us to understand the sadness behind problematic behaviours. Until we can truly understand the grief occurring in our blended family, we are tempted to read the actions that follow as mere misbehaviour.

Compassion recognizes the suffering of others and feels the hurt along with them. It does not stand above, so that it can judge and condescend; nor does it stand below, so it can cower and be afraid. Kindness stands beside someone and wants to help.

COMPASSION FOR THE PAST

Most kids in stepfamilies have been through a great deal of pain. The less time that the children have had to heal, the harder it will be for them. If they were not given any resources to help them, they may well be still hurting years later. Time does not heal all wounds, at least not without some other tools helping it along. Studies show that children are still affected by divorce, even into adulthood.[2]

What can we as stepmoms do to show compassion? First, we can have an open heart and to let their pain into our hearts. We can recognize that acting out is often a sign of unresolved grief.

We can listen to them, get to know them, accept them and forgive them. We can appreciate the battle they have been through in losing their family.

Parenting a child who has lost their mother to death takes a special kind of compassion. As a stepmother to a grieving child, you can play a significant part in helping that child heal.

My friend Sherry is a stepmother who stepped into her children's lives after their mother had passed away. She refers to herself as "Mom," and the children give her that title, too.

Her situation, like so many, is complex. Of the five children she became stepmother to, the oldest girl passed away at age 20, and the youngest one stayed with a relative. The remaining three children were six, three, and two years old when she entered their lives.

When I asked her how a stepmom could help deal with the grief of the children, Sherry shared these powerful words:

 Be kind, be understanding, be humble, and listen

to the children with an open heart and mind. They may talk about their mom: please be okay with that; it's what they need to do. Let them feel their mom with them still.

Sherry's advice contains wisdom for all stepmoms. Have an open heart and mind, and let the children be themselves. Acknowledge that they may still be hurting, and don't judge them.

A sense of empathy goes a long way towards building trust with those that are hurting. Just being there and caring is powerful. You don't have to say a lot; just be present.

COMPASSION CAN BE CHALLENGING

As much as we may try to show compassion, it can be difficult, at times. We may think of ourselves as loving people but struggle to truly open our hearts. There are valid reasons that compassion can be challenging. Sometimes, kindness must be tempered with boundaries and limits.

First of all, giving from the heart can be emotionally draining. It is especially draining when it is not reciprocated. So, we can have compassion, but we also need to set limits and protect ourselves, too.

Compassion can also be challenging because we may think of it as making excuses for someone. Therefore, it is important to remember that showing compassion does not mean having no limits or guidelines.

It can also be difficult because someone else's suffering may bring memories of our own. It may trigger uncomfortable feelings about our past and bring up unhealed memories. If we have told ourselves that we weren't hurt in the past, acknowledging someone else's hurt may take our guard down.

The most potent reason that compassion is difficult for us, as stepmoms, is that we are scared of being hurt. It is hard to be open with individuals who may seem to dislike us, sometimes even hate us. Sometimes compassion means caring for someone without an expectation of receiving love in return. It is for this reason that compassion must sometimes be balanced with boundaries and protecting our own hearts, too.

HAVE COMPASSION ON YOURSELF

Finally, remember that these gifts apply not just to the kids, but to you and your spouse, as well. I encourage you to have compassion towards all members of your family. Your spouse may still be hurting, too, from the losses he endured.

It is certain that he is not always sure of how to handle all the situations that come up in trying to blend a family. He is likely torn between loyalty for his new wife, dedication to his children, and demands from his former partner.

He might do strange things that puzzle you because of the grief he is still enduring over the loss of his family. He may be having emotions impossible to speak out aloud and reactions that he does not understand.

Just as importantly, have compassion for yourself. You have never been a stepmom before. There are no rules to follow.

You didn't take a course on this in high school. Take it easy on yourself.

The stepmother's role is often fraught with rejection, confusion and misunderstanding. In many ways, you have lost control of your world, which can be scary. Don't judge yourself too harshly if you react more emotionally than you think you should. Be patient with yourself and take time to care for yourself.

COMPASSION IS THE BASKET

To end this chapter, I want to share a story from my childhood. When I was ten years old, I remember getting a severe case of mononucleosis, or "kissing disease." It was very contagious, so my parents kept me home from school for nearly two weeks. It was a miserable condition that makes you tired, achy and weak.

My week got much better when my grandma showed up at the door with a very inviting gift basket! She drove two hours to deliver a basket full of chocolate bars, a puzzle, and many other goodies.

There is something so personal about a care package in a basket. Can you imagine a care package in a plain cardboard box? It definitely would not have the same effect. In fact, the basket itself is often the most valuable part of the offering, lasting beyond the perishables of tea sachets and jars of jam.

I remember the basket itself was so pretty and lasted longer than most of the gifts that it contained. The basket *was* one of the gifts – but it also held all the other presents that my grandmother had brought me.

In conclusion, compassion is a lot like that basket because it is the *container* that will hold all of the other gifts we will look at in this book. From a heart of compassion, we give acceptance, patience, forgiveness and endurance, and all the other gifts.

4

THE GIFT OF ACCEPTANCE

*D*id you know that the great president Abraham Lincoln was a stepchild? When he was just nine years old, he lost his mother, Nancy Hicks Lincoln, to a plague called "milk sickness."

A year after his mother's death, his father remarried a young widow named Sarah Bush Johnston. Sarah took this lost family into her heart and restored order to the run-down cabin.[1] Later in life, Lincoln called his stepmom "his best friend in this world," and said that "no son could love a mother more than he loves her."[2]

What did Sarah give little Abraham? She accepted him! Her stepson was intellectual instead of practical. Instead of attending to the chores, he gave mock speeches and read books.[3] His distaste for duties led to beatings from his father.[4]

Being different, he was insecure and lacked confidence.[5] His loving stepmother felt a sense of kinship with him, even though she herself was not educated. She is quoted as saying, "His mind and mine, what little I had, seemed to run together, more in the same channel."[6] She sought to understand him, brought him books, and nurtured his desire to get at the exact meaning of words.[7]

Can you imagine if Lincoln had not had his stepmother in his life? If not for the approval of this obscure woman, living in the sticks of America, his latent potential may have never been realized. Her love made all the difference in the world to this young boy. Writer John Widmer summarizes her immense influence in this way:

> If Lincoln saved the Union, she saved him. At just the right moment, she encountered a small motherless boy and helped him to become Abraham Lincoln.[8]

ACCEPTANCE IS EVERYTHING

To feel truly affirmed by another human being is what we all long for. Acceptance is unconditional love. It says the other person is good enough, just as they are. They don't have to change to please us. They don't have to prove themselves or earn our approval.

The wife longs to be loved unconditionally by her husband. Children desire to be accepted by their parents. We all want to feel welcomed; the need for belonging is one of the most basic psychological needs.

One of my favourite writers, Paul Tournier, goes so far as to say that acceptance goes to the very core of who we are:

> At the heart of personality is the need to feel a sense of being lovable without having to qualify for that acceptance.[9]

In other words, we learn who we are when others accept us. Highly respected psychologist and author Dr. Thomas Gordon echoes these thoughts:

> When a person feels that he is truly accepted by another, as he is, then he is freed to move from there and to begin to think about how he wants to change, how he wants to grow, how he can become different, how he might become more of what he is capable of being.
>
> Acceptance is like the fertile soil that permits a tiny seed to develop into the lovely flower it is capable of becoming."[10]

The doctor says that loving a person unconditionally gives them the freedom to make better choices. This, in turn, leads to them growing into who they are meant to be. Isn't this so true? We remember those in our lives who make us feel "good enough" and it motivates us to be even better.

STEPCHILDREN OFTEN REJECT US

The story of Abraham Lincoln is inspiring because it shows the tremendous impact that a stepmother can have. It is wonderful to hear of a stepmom who was so appreciated and loved.

You might find the story a bit discouraging, though, if your situation seems nothing like Sarah's. Maybe you have tried to accept your stepson, but he wants nothing to do with *you.*

First of all, be aware that, in most cases, it won't always be like this. Learning to adjust is a long process. Renowned stepfamily expert Patricia Papernow estimates that this process takes anywhere from four to twelve years.[11] In the meantime, though, it can be devastating and make you feel like quitting. Please remember that all of this is part of the process of becoming a family.

SPECIFIC FORMS OF ACCEPTANCE

We agree that the gift of acceptance is a powerful one, but how does this gift play out, practically speaking? Here are five specific areas in which we can show approval to the children in our lives.

1. **Be welcoming.** The first way we can be accepting towards someone is to behave as if we were glad to see them. When we see our stepchildren after time apart, we can welcome them with our eyes, our smile and our words. We can show excitement and hug them if they are willing.

2. **Accept their emotions.** When someone is grieving, they

long to be accepted, however the pain manifests itself. This means recognizing problematic behaviour for what it often is: grief talking. Acceptance also calls you to forgive, perhaps often.

Accepting emotions means that we are not dismissive of how someone is feeling. We do not expect them to ignore their feelings and act like everything is okay when it really isn't. In other words, we don't require them to put on a mask.

3. **Accept their personalities.** Embracing an individual's personality differences is another way to show acceptance. Many arguments in family life can be stopped when we stop expecting others to behave exactly as we would. Sometimes kids (and our partners) handle things radically differently than we would because their temperament is opposite to ours.

To give an example, my husband and I are complete opposites. He is a bubbly extrovert. I am a sensitive introvert. He is a natural jock. I am a clumsy bookworm. When we first got together, I wondered how we would ever survive all our disparities. It turns out that his kids were opposite from me in many ways, too. (They were *his* kids, after all!)

Introverts and extroverts see the world very differently. Extroverts need social time like a plant needs water. If they are left alone for too long, they may start to act out. Oppositely, an introvert can become undone if they don't get some time alone during the day.

If your stepchild is an introvert and you're not, be patient with his desire to get away, and don't take it personally. If he is more extroverted than you, don't judge his need for attention as immaturity but see it as a need for his temperament.

For more on the topic of accepting your stepchildren's personality differences, check out a guest blog post I wrote for the blog, *Stepmom Help:*

https://www.stepmomhelp.com/guest-post-by-sharilee-swaity-personality-differences-in-the-stepfamily/[12]

4. Accept their interests. Another way of showing acceptance to your stepchildren is to accept their interests. Getting to know the passions of young people is a compelling way of connecting with them.

As a teacher, I've built relationships with many different students with a wide variety of enthusiasms. Showing curiosity and asking genuine questions has helped me bridge the gap with pupils very different from myself. It has been fascinating to learn from them!

You may struggle to discover the interests of your stepchildren but look for clues and you may be surprised at what you can find out. Observe their belongings, including the toys or games they use most often. Watch to see what they are viewing on YouTube.

As a teacher for many years, I have kept close tabs on what kids are into. If you would like a detailed list of possible kid interests, sign up here to have it sent to you:

https://secondmarriage.xyz/kids-interests-inventory-33344

5. Accept their weaknesses. The final way of accepting a child is to take his shortcomings and help him see his weaknesses as strengths. How do *we* do this, in practical terms? Let me give an example to demonstrate.

Let's say that the child is continually moving and can't sit still. In certain situations, like church or school, this can be a deterrent from behaving appropriately. Too much movement can also be due to a learning disability and require other modifications.

View his high energy as being a strength and find ways to channel it. Go to the playground together or visit a trampoline park. If the child is young, you could pretend to be an Olympic judge giving him high scores on his brilliant moves.

Most weaknesses come with associated strengths. Learning disabilities often come with incredible imaginations. Aggression comes with courage. Reactiveness comes with enhanced sensitivity and awareness. Focusing on strong areas goes a long way toward building confidence and resilience.

ACCEPTANCE IS POWERFUL

In conclusion, accepting the children in our lives is a powerful approach for breaking down barriers. When we accept them before they accept us, we open the door to them feeling safe and putting down their guard.

5

THE GIFT OF PATIENCE

Do you ever watch those fixer-upper shows on HGTV? It's intoxicating to watch dumps being transformed into shining masterpieces. Sometimes in the span of a week or even a weekend! Home renovation shows are a guilty pleasure I find hard to resist!

You know how they go. Walls are torn out, dated cupboards come down, and the new ones come in. They purchase the latest vanity, new flooring, furniture, and pillows to match. It all adds up to the big reveal at the end. Everyone oohs and ahhs, and we are amazed once again at the incredible design.

Wow! It can be inspirational! There is a dark side to all that perfection, though. Sometimes we expect our houses (and lives) to match up to the shows we see on TV.

In our stepfamilies, there can be a similar temptation: to want to make things better way too quickly. To push for changes we know would fix up the place so much.

Maybe we wish the kids didn't play so many video games or eat so much junk food. We see Dad making all these parenting mistakes and we want to help! We desperately long for close relationships and wish the tension would disappear.

We may have an ideal in our mind of what a family is supposed to look like and feel more frustrated every day that reality is so very far from our imagination. Having patience is a gift for both ourselves and our family.

PATIENCE SCALES DOWN EXPECTATIONS

During the first few years of being a stepmom, I could have used a lot more patience. I had an ideal family in my mind, where we all got along and loved on each other. In my perfect scenario, the kids were reading books instead of playing video games. We all felt a sense of closeness. I felt like *part* of the family, not an outsider.

In my frustration, I lacked patience. I wanted things to change *now*! What I didn't take into account was that relationships take a lifetime to build. Having more patience would have helped me scale down my expectations and be grateful for baby steps.

Later on I learned about how different stepfamilies are from original families, and realized that our struggles had been completely typical. Stepfamilies are harder, more complicated and just overall messier than biological families. There are far more issues to work through, and that is why "gelling" as a stepfamily is definitely a long-term project!

Let's examine some of the reasons that blended families are so much more complicated. When we examine all these factors, it is easy to see why it will take time to work through all of it.

- As a stepparent you have a comparatively short history with the children, unlike the biological parents, who have been with them from the beginning. This lack of history makes it harder for them to trust you and bond with you.
- You do not have the legal authority to make crucial decisions regarding the child. Although you're doing the work of caretaking, you can feel like more of a babysitter than a parent.
- Your life is directly affected by the attitude and actions of your stepchild's other mother. If she has an issue with you, it will likely make it difficult for the child to get close to you.
- Your partner is forced to have a relationship with his ex-wife, whether he likes it or not. This continued contact with a former partner can make it harder to heal and move on.
- You are also forced to have a relationship with her, as well, which can be awkward and painful, especially if there is conflict.
- Money is more complex, because there are often support payments coming in or out of the home, which are usually dictated by the legal system. It is

more complex to figure out who pays for what and where the money will be spent.

- Dads often parent out of guilt, and are afraid to be too strict, in case they lose their kids even more.
- Emotions in a stepfamily are more complex, too. Because of the loss that always precedes the formation of a blended family, whether through divorce or bereavement, grief is usually there, even if it goes unnoticed.

FEELING LIKE AN OUTSIDER

There are many complications that a blended family endures, but the biggest and most profound challenge comes from the very structure of the family itself.

The truth is that kids and their biological parents have a pre-existing bond that will often make the non-biological parent feel like they don't belong. This bond automatically makes the newcomer, the stepparent, feel like an outsider. The bio parent will then feel torn between his kids and his partner.

In her book *Surviving and Thriving in Stepfamily Relationships: What Works and What Doesn't,* respected stepfamily researcher Dr. Patricia Papernow labels this phenomena as "Stuck Insider/Stuck Outsider."[1] She describes the stepparent as the "stuck outsider" because she is *stuck* on the outside of the child-parent relationship. The original parent is the "stuck insider," because he is *stuck* between his children and his partner.

Papernow explains that both partners are continually

disappointed because they experience two different realities simultaneously: one as outsider and the other as insider. Their experiences within the family are so widely different that they find it hard to relate to each other.

Does any of that sound familiar? This frustrating dynamic is the most profound reason that patience is required. With patience, you are better able to see that the tension everyone feels is just part of the process. Slowly building up connections, as we talk about in this book, will, in many cases, help ease the conflict and create less of a divide over time.

THE FIXER-UPPER

My husband and I bought a home four years ago and it could lovingly be called a fixer-upper." On my most frustrated days, I would call it a handyman's special. The place needs a fair amount of work, to put it mildly. So far, there have been no calls from talented television hosts offering to do the house over in a weekend. So, we must rely on patience!

Each repair and every renovation will take funds – funds that we must save for carefully. And we live in the imperfection. Living this way takes patience and an attitude of working on it bit by bit.

So it is with your stepfamily. There are no Chip and Joanna Gaines of blended families who will come and make everything look fabulous in two weeks. No, instead, we must put in work day by day, sometimes minute by minute.

6

THE GIFT OF FORGIVENESS

*F*ive winters ago, on a frigid Sunday night, I stayed late in my classroom preparing my lessons for the week to come. When I was done the ground was covered in fresh snow, which was still coming down steadily.

I drove home slowly, feeling the vehicle slip on the icy surface several times. I cautiously inched along, unable to see because of the blowing snow.

When I went to take the sharp turn into our community, the Chevrolet 4 x 4 truck slipped on the ice, turned upside down and landed in the ditch. Because my speed had been so slow and there was lots of soft snow, the cab was not crushed. I was fine but the truck did not survive nearly as well as I did.

When my husband and I went to examine the vehicle in the tow truck facility the next day, we knew our beloved truck was doomed for the junkyard. This was sad because this particular make and model was no longer on the market, and it worked especially well for us and our country lifestyle.

After everything settled down, I thought about how the truck had been my husband's baby. I felt apprehensive that he might start to feel angry towards me for destroying our vehicle. (I vividly recall my uncle yelling at my aunt for hours one night, for a mere fender bender, so my expectations were based on experience.)

I told my husband how sorry I was and was truly amazed at his response. He told me not to be ridiculous, and that he was just so glad I was okay. During the next few months, as we dealt with insurance adjusters and shopped for something different to drive, I never once heard any resentment for taking away something that he really valued.

Forgiveness is one of the qualities that I treasure in the man that I married. His forgiveness does not always come quickly or automatically but I feel confident knowing he will not hold a long-term grudge. Through the years, I've seen him forgive others, too, who have hurt him or done him wrong.

FORGIVENESS IS HARD

Forgiveness is one of the hardest things we are asked to do as human beings. When someone wrongs us, we feel violated and have a desire to protect ourselves. Often, there is also a part of us that wants the other party to feel some of the hurt that we feel, in the interest of justice and fairness.

As stepmoms, it is almost guaranteed that you will have occasion to forgive, likely many times. As we learned in the previous chapter, it is the very structure of stepfamilies that leads to hurt feelings and estrangement, especially at the beginning. The gift of forgiveness can help us see past slights and careless words slung out in the painful process of becoming a family.

Understanding stepfamily dynamics helps us see that in most cases, it's really not about us. So much problematic behaviour is about a stepchild losing his family and dealing with all the changes that go with that. Lashing out is often a symptom of deep hurt and confusion, often directed at the outsider, the stepparent.

Many of the hurtful reactions of our step kids can also be attributed to the reality of something called *loyalty binds*. "Loyalty bind" is a term used to refer to the conflict that kids often feel when getting close to a stepparent feels like a betrayal to their mother.

This can lead to erratic behaviour, where a child can start to seem close to you, but then suddenly pull away and distance himself. As soon as he starts to like you even a little bit, he may panic and feel like he is being disloyal to his mother.

Another reason that kids may resent you in their lives is that you're a constant reminder that their parents are not getting back together. As well, your presence means that they no longer have exclusive access to their father. Finally, you are unfamiliar and do things differently than their mom.

Knowing that the lashing out you are getting from them is due to all of the complex dynamics makes it so much easier to forgive. None of these reasons have anything to do with you personally. Instead, they are a rejection of the situation.

WHAT EXACTLY IS FORGIVENESS?

But what exactly *is* forgiveness? One of my favourite definitions is the following:

> Forgiveness: To give up resentment against or stop wanting to punish (someone) for an offense or fault; pardon.[1]

There are two parts to this definition: giving up resentment and giving up the need to punish our offender. Neither one of these is easy.

Resentment can start to fester quietly inside of us when we see a wrong done against us. It is easy to feel resentment but the problem is that it builds into bitterness, and it makes it hard to love anyone or be happy about anything.

To forgive someone is very similar to pardoning someone. When a criminal is pardoned, it doesn't mean he didn't commit the crime. Forgiveness does not mean that we are saying someone did not do wrong. The very fact that forgiveness is needed means there was some wrong done.

Sometimes forgiveness will not happen all at once. It can be a process, and sometimes we are too hurt to be able to do it. As well, forgiveness does not mean we can necessarily get close to the person. Sometimes we need to protect our hearts and keep our distance. Finally, forgiveness does not make us weak.

In fact, being able to let things go is the ultimate sign of strength.

Most importantly, forgiveness is not just a gift for others; it is also a gift to yourself. By forgiving, you free yourself to keep loving and save yourself from a world of bitterness and defeat.

7

THE GIFT OF ENCOURAGEMENT

*J*onny Winters' father passed away before he turned six and his mother married another man. Because he and his brother were so young when they lost their dad, both of them took on their stepdad as a father.

This little boy, born in the early 1950s, would often get his words mixed up, which caused him to get flustered and stutter. Every time that little Jonny scrambled his words, this stepfather would ask, "Are you stupid?"

Jonny's brother, Steve, says his stepfather was not a malicious man; he just didn't understand children. He didn't know the right things to say.

What none of them knew was that Jonny had a little-known condition called dyslexia. His brain worked differently. An astute teacher in third grade got him a diagnosis, and more importantly, told him he was not"stupid."

His stepfather did not realize he was planting bad seeds in this little boy's heart: words that were difficult to erase.

Just as Jonny heard words that would take a lifetime to overcome, so can positive, affirming words leave an impact that will last forever. When we plant seeds of encouragement and affirmation into our loved one's hearts, we are building up the souls and minds in our care.

The dictionary defines *encouragement* as "the action of giving someone support, confidence, or hope."[1] Encouragement is something all of us crave, and we can never get too much of it.

Words are powerful, for the good or the bad. Years later, we remember words spoken to us but long forgotten by the one who said it in an off-the-cuff moment. Our hearts long to hear good words about ourselves, our accomplishments, even our appearance. We long to be told that we are loved, respected, liked.

All children need and crave these types of words. As a stepmother, you're a very important person in their lives. Your words can bring life.

What an influential position we hold in our loved ones' lives when we sow words of encouragement into their minds.

PRACTICAL STRATEGIES

There are many ways you can give the gift of encouragement to the children in your life. Here is a list of four practical ways you can bless your stepchild through your words.

1. Notice when she does well and point out how gifted she in this area. Be specific in your praise. This could be anything, from a tendency to be tidy, to knowing how to fix things, to being a fast reader. Take notice and mention it, more than once.

2. Thank her when she does things around the house and takes on responsibilities. Notice when she shows consideration and respect, and show genuine gratitude. Even if a child is consistently faithful in duties, don't take it for granted.

3. Another effective method of affirmation that is less direct is called "secondhand praise." In earshot of the person mention to someone else (your spouse, other family member or friend) something awesome about them. You might say, "Sarah is so athletic!" or "Did you hear about how well Chris did on his math test?"

Secondhand praise can be especially effective if you don't feel the relationship is at a point where you can share appreciation with the child directly. If they have a wall up, making communication difficult, saying it to someone else lets them hear it but does not require a response from them. It has the advantage of sharing that sense of honour with others, too.

4. Another way to help give support is through the written word. This, too, can be an easier way to communicate if you are still struggling to have conversations. Buy a little card and

put it in her bedroom, saying you're thinking of her. You can also be creative with it. Little girls, especially, love stickers, so add a few that you think she would like. Draw a silly picture if you feel inclined.

Kids love to receive texts or other messages on social media. This is a fun, casual method of communication and the one with which most teens feel comfortable.

5. Encouragement is often associated with helping to motivate someone. In fact, another definition of *encouragement* is "words or behaviour that give someone confidence to do something."[2]

Our positive words help others believe that they can accomplish a task, endure hardship or reach a goal. Kids are often going through hard times, whether at school or at home. If your stepchild is discouraged about something that happened at school or another environment, listen with patience. Then assure her with words such as "You got this!" or "You will get through this."

If your relationship is open enough, you can help build them up by sharing your own story with them, too. Tell how you handled a bully at school or overcame a learning disability. Sometimes just hearing that someone else went through a situation is encouraging. We all love to know that we are not alone.

YOU MIGHT MAKE ALL THE DIFFERENCE

To end, I want to share about a very encouraging person that influenced *me* greatly: my mother. My mother did not have an easy life but no matter her problems, she always had an encouraging word for someone else.

When she passed away at age 54, there were many people at her funeral that we did not expect to see. I have no proof, but I suspect they were there because my mother had had an encouraging conversation with them, one on one, and they came to show their appreciation

She was always reaching out. At my cousin's funeral, who had committed suicide at age 17, my mom began talking to my cousin's classmates who were devastated at the loss of their friend. No one had asked her to speak to these brokenhearted teens — she simply saw a need and started pouring out her words of love. She did that wherever she went..

Not everyone in my family was as affirming as my mother. Growing up, I witnessed and experienced verbal and emotional abuse.

I was a very sensitive child and the harsh words penetrated deep into my psyche. As a teenager, I angrily questioned my worth and often experienced suicidal thoughts. In the midst of the turmoil, one voice helped get me through: my mother's. She poured out words of affirmation and grace on me and my sister constantly.

She was generous with her praise and her love was sunshine coming into my soul. I felt ugly, but she told me I was beautiful. I felt useless, but she told me I was gifted. I felt hopeless, but she told me there was hope.

All my life, I struggled with confidence. My mother's words sustained me in the battle against low self-esteem and doubt.

It took me longer than my peers to achieve my goals. I made a lot of mistakes looking for love in all the wrong places, but my mother's powerful words of encouragement never left me.

Finally, years later, I started to believe for myself. I was beautiful. I was gifted. I did have a future.

Never underestimate the power of *your* uplifting words. There's a good chance you won't be thanked directly. It may take years before there is fruit but have faith that you are planting seeds of goodness that will last a lifetime.

My mother passed away before she saw me realize many of her dreams, but she influences me greatly to this day. Never forget that you are in a position of influence in your family. Your words might be the words that make all the difference in the world to one person.

8

THE GIFT OF LISTENING

*H*ave you ever met someone who listened to you like you were the only person in the room? Do you remember how you felt with this person? Being listened to makes us feel safe, important and cherished.

Listening is a lost art in our technology-driven society. The act of focusing on what someone else is saying, without distractions, can go a long way. An open ear sends the message that someone is important to you.

So many of us (including me!) are addicted to the sheer convenience of our devices and computers. We are so busy looking at our phone, checking our Facebook and texting our friends that we forget to pay attention to those who are right in front of us.

In today's climate, listening is so compelling because it is so rare. Give the gift of listening to the kid in your life. Put down your phone and have a real conversation. Get to know him. Look him in the eyes.

LISTENING BUILDS CONNECTION

Listening with an unbiased ear is one of the best ways you can connect with someone. It is an act of love. Spend time having conversations with the children in your life. Get to know them — their opinions and their interests. There is no shortcut to getting to know someone: you must put in the time. Conversation is an art that you can share with the next generation.

One of the significant ways that I was able to connect with my stepson was to listen. He was a teenager, and his world was video games, swords and hanging out with his friends. We didn't share many common interests, but I really got to know him, just by listening.

He was also still hurting from his family situation, and he needed to talk. Being there meant not judging him but being a calm voice in the chaos.

LISTENING HELPS TO HEAL

When my mother passed away, I wanted to talk about her to whoever would listen. To express my feelings, I wrote a poem titled "Do You Wanna Talk About Her?" If you would like to see this poem published online, you can view it here:

https://letterpile.com/poetry/I-Wanna-Talk- About-Her

Here are the first few lines:

Do you want to talk about her
Every minute of the day?
Do you always think about her
When you walk and when you pray?
Do you grieve the day she left us
With a constant aching song?
Do you call out with a fresh cry
When you realize she is gone?

In this poem, I am asking the reader if they want to talk about my mother, as I do, every "minute of the day." When we are dealing with someone who is grieving, the need to talk is imperative.

Suzy Yehl Marta, founder of the Rainbows program for grieving children, states that people need to repeat their story a total of at least *30* times before they can safely move on.[1] Studies confirm that children able to talk about their loss do better long-term.[2]

Studies show that children from divorced families have many unanswered questions and turmoil from the separation. Often, they find it difficult to ask their parents their questions, for fear of hurting their feelings.[3]

As a stepmom, don't underestimate your value in being a neutral party for your stepchildren. In this case, your status as an "outsider" can be an advantage because you're considered less biased. You can listen to their concerns and experiences without taking it as personally as their parents would.

It is crucial that, as you listen, you remain as neutral as possible. It is well-documented that parents often find it hard to relate to their kids during a time of grief, such as divorce or bereavement, because of having to deal with their own feelings about the situation.[4] When you listen without judgment, you can give a child a place to vent.

66 In order to really understand, we need to listen, not reply. We need to listen long and attentively.[5]

— PAUL TOURNIER

TIPS FOR EFFECTIVE LISTENING

Listening might sound simple but it can be challenging. Here are some suggestions for listening more effectively:

1. **Listen fully.** Don't think about what you're going to say next. Instead, become fully engaged in simply understanding what the other person is saying, without worrying about what comes next. Listen to understand.

2. **Listen actively.** Practice something called "active listening,"especially if you're talking about something emotional. This is a technique that our counsellor taught us in marriage therapy. After the person is done speaking, probe gently by asking questions to make sure you understand what they are saying.

This is called "paraphrasing," where you clarify that you have heard the other person. You can use phrases such as "Do you mean ..." or "So I understand that you are saying..." Listen until they are done speaking and expressing what they are trying to say, and then respond by making sure you really understood what they were saying.

3. **Listen honestly.** When you're listening, be honest and don't automatically agree with everything they say. Be willing to challenge them gently with your own thoughts and ideas on the topic.

Don't be argumentative by insisting you are right. Instead, bring up your ideas as "yours," not automatically the right ideas. It is a balance between being sensitive and honest. By disagreeing sometimes, it shows that you're not a fake!

4. **Listen humbly.** Don't act like you know everything, especially when it comes to talking about more neutral topics such as your stepchild's interests. Be curious and open to what they can teach you. Ask questions to show your curiosity, even if it is a topic that is not generally on your radar.

5. **Listen intelligently.** Listen with your mind, as well as your heart. In other words, hear what they are saying and see how it matches up with what you already know. Then, add to the conversation and the listener's education. After your communication, you may even want to look for more information on the topic so that you can add to your ongoing dialogue.

9

THE GIFT OF SPACE

*E*arly in our marriage, my husband and I bought a modest mobile home. The structure had two tiny bedrooms and a slightly larger master. The rooms were hardly big enough for a twin bed and a small dresser.

The boys lived with us every second weekend, and we made the decision to give each of them a bedroom of their own. As much as I longed for an office, I thought giving each boy a retreat was paramount. The boys were 12 and 14, the age when kids get their own bedroom.

On the days they weren't there, the rooms sat empty, and I caught myself dreaming of extra storage or a nice lounge area. I knew, though, we had made the right choice in giving them a space of their own. If sibling rivalry started to get heated (which it invariably did) or someone just needed time to think, they each had a place get away and chill for a while.

PART TIME STEPMOMS WITHOUT KIDS

For part-time stepmoms without their own kids, custody creates a strange rhythm within a family. It is like you have two lives: your quiet time without the children, and your experience with the children.

Your time without them is calmer and more predictable, and then it's a few days of chaos! Everyone has to adjust once again, and the first few hours can tend to be a bit awkward.

One way to help calm things down is to try to allow everyone a space for themselves, if at all possible. Even if it is not a whole room, try to have a place that is theirs: perhaps a cubby hole or a dresser.

A sense of ownership and boundaries is essential to help the kids feel comfortable. The children are not visitors – they are residents! Act like they live there and are not acquaintances.

FULL TIME STEPMOMS

If the children live with you full-time, it is even more important that the children have space to call their own. Separate bedrooms are not always possible but there needs to be some place that is distinctly theirs. Adequate space helps give ownership to children.

When my husband and I took full-time custody of one of the boys, we moved into a bigger home. Our growing teenager had nearly the entire basement to himself. He loved bringing his gang of friends over to goof off in the space, and the good part is the ceiling was soundproof!

As much as possible, it is crucial that everyone gets some space of their own, and this includes you. When we changed residences, I was thrilled to gain a dedicated office area where I could get away from it all.

Space not only refers to bedrooms. The whole house needs to accommodate all members of the family, both full- or part-**time.** This can be a big adjustment for everyone.

Living with kids might mean toys in the living room or an XBox in the spare room. The gift of space makes sure that everyone feels like the house is theirs, including you. This is not always an easy balance to strike, but well worth the effort.

STEPMOMS WITH THEIR OWN KIDS

For families who are blending two sets of siblings together, the space issue is even more complex, and the need of boundaries even more important. You need to create space so that all the kids have some space from the adults and from each other.

You may have children coming and going at different times to other households. In this case, you want to be sure that everyone feels treated fairly and has somewhere that is uniquely theirs.

If one set of kids lives there full-time, while another set lives there part-time, be sure to make the part-time ones feel like they have a say in how the house is arranged, too.

Have rules in place that ensure everyone's privacy is respected, especially when it comes to changing. Bathrooms can be an issue, so make sure you have enough washrooms that everyone feels comfortable. Consider some bathroom scheduling so that everyone gets a chance to do their personal grooming in peace.

EMOTIONAL SPACE

The gift of space not only refers to actual physical space within a home but also emotional space. Giving someone space means keeping a safe distance until they are ready to be closer.

You can give your stepchildren space by not trying to get too close all at once. Becoming a family will not happen quickly. In fact, it usually takes years. Respecting boundaries means not forcing conversations. It also means not pushing for a false sense of intimacy.

As stepmoms, we are behaving as moms. We make dinner, clean the house, and drive them places. It is so easy to cross the line and start to feel like we *are* the mom. If the child does not feel the same way, though, it can make everyone uncomfortable if we get too familiar. However close we may start to feel, we must always remember that they already have a mother.

GIVE YOURSELF SPACE, TOO

Remember that there will be times that the gift of space is for *you*. There may be seasons when you need to withdraw and protect yourself.

Sometimes taking care of yourself means setting up firmer boundaries. This might mean insisting that one room in the house is only for you and not for everyone else. Or it might mean standing up to your husband when he makes plans without consulting you first.

It can also mean stepping away from the situation if the stepchildren are not accepting of you. In order for a gift to be appreciated, it must be received. If they are not ready to receive you, sometimes you need to distance yourself. You still care, but you are protecting your heart.

In conclusion, the gift of space is about making room for the children who have entered your life and saving some room for yourself, too.

10

THE GIFT OF DADDY TIME

When I first started spending time with my stepsons, I was acutely aware that I was a new person in their lives. I did not want to push myself on them too quickly. After all, their dad and I were the ones forming a relationship, and they were along for the ride. I didn't want them to feel it had been imposed on them.

When we went for walks or activities, I would try to not *always* hold Vern's hand, but let them walk beside him, too. I would often walk on the outside when we were together so that they did not feel supplanted.

I didn't want them to feel that suddenly I was in the right-hand space, next to Vern, as if I was "bumping them out." Sometimes I sensed that they were craving "Daddy Time," and tried to give them more space. This meant letting them do activities together, without me joining.

DISPELLING THE EVIL STEPMOTHER FEAR

One of the greatest fears that children of single dads have is that they will no longer be able to spend time with their father when a new woman comes along. From this foreboding, comes the stereotype of the "evil stepmother."

Many fairytales feature a stepmother who is threatened by the stepchild who comes with their newly formed relationship. Then, they make plans to get the child out of the way, so they can have their new spouse all to themselves. Cinderella's stepmom banishes her to the attic, while Snow White's literally sends her out to be killed off.

Respecting the need for "Daddy Time" is a powerful way to signal that you are not there to take over and get the children out of the way. Instead, it is the very opposite. You are there to support the critical relationship with their father.

Research reveals that mothers are still the ones who most often get custody of their children.[1] Therefore, most children of divorce or separation end up losing a full-time father.

When you come along, they may feel like this already scarce resource is being threatened. It is quite possible that their father is spending some of the time he used to spend with his children with you.

Even if a you're all spending time together, separate "Daddy Time" is still essential. We all feel more comfortable with those that we know best. Therefore, the children need time alone to keep that relationship active.

It is a delicate balance. On the one hand, you are trying to get closer to your stepchildren by spending time with them. On the other hand, you know they need time alone with their dad.

Dispel the "evil stepmother" myth by encouraging your spouse to spend time alone with his kids. Use this time to go and do your own thing. Give them some space and respect their relationship.

Consider things from your stepchild's perspective. She has already gone through the loss of the family she always knew. Watching her father marry someone else means that her old family is never coming back.

She needs concrete assurance that the relationship with her father is solid. This is especially true if he is a part-time dad. She needs to know that you're not there to take her parent from her. She needs "Daddy Time," and she always will.

11

THE GIFT OF TRADITION

*I*n the early 1990s, Sister Mary Agnes Dombrowski was sent to work with challenged children at a place called the St. Charles Children's Home. The centre took in behaviourally challenged children and gave them a home.[1]

As a child, the nun had never even babysat, so this assignment was especially challenging for her. Now, she found herself working with troubled kids. She confesses that if the girls had not killed one another by the end of the day, she considered it a success!

Until she met one little girl who changed her mind, Sister Agnes doubted her work was making any difference. This particular child spent her first day at the home swearing, kicking, spitting, screaming and hitting the other children.

By the time evening came around, the sister wondered how

she was going to survive. Exhausted, she and her coworker showed the girl her bed, tucked her in, and said their prayers with her. This was the routine they practiced daily with all the children.

After their evening ritual, Agnes sat beside the little girl's bed in a rocking chair and watched her go to sleep. She wanted to make sure that the child did not get up and start hitting the other children again.

After a couple of minutes, the child looked up at her and said the words that would change the nun's life. "Sister Mary Agnes, this is my first safe night." This was the first time Mary Agnes was able to see past the behaviours that were so problematic and recognize a hurting child.

The next day, the nun was surprised to hear from the counsellor at the girl's school. The professional told her that every day, that little girl had been sent to the therapist's office. Upon arriving, she would grab a doll and beat that toy mercilessly.

This day, however, the little girl asked if she could play something different. She asked the counsellor to lay down on a table and covered her with a blanket. She then said "This is how Sister Mary Agnes tucks me in." From that day forward, her therapy sessions started with some form of playing "Sister Mary Agnes."

The game consisted of role playing the "tuck in" or some other routine that the sisters practiced at the home. Those small little gestures, tucking her in, and saying night-time prayers, done almost automatically, became the lifeline for this little girl to start to feel safe and normal. If you would like to watch this video for yourself, you can see it at the link below:

https://www.youtube.com/watch?v=beNIT5qXxvo

HONOUR THE OLD WAYS

When children go through a life trauma, the disruption to their routines is one of the biggest challenges. Nothing feels normal, anymore. According to the American Psychological Association, routine plays a vital role in healing from traumatic events:

> Helping children, families, and communities reestablish routines and roles can help return normalcy to a child's life, providing reassurance and a sense of safety. Resuming regular mealtimes and bedtimes, returning to school, renewing friendships and leisure activities, and playing in a safe environment can all help in this regard.[2]

In other words, helping to make a child's world as familiar as possible is one of the keys to helping the child get over difficult and painful events. Children of divorce or bereavement have already endured a multitude of changes. It is easy to lose many of their family traditions. When one parent is gone, it is hard to maintain the usual way of doing things. Change is inevitable, but this is a big loss. Older children, especially, can feel it even more because they have had more years of traditions to miss.

Remarriage can seem like an even further threat to keeping those traditions alive. The stepmom is a new person, unaware of how things "have always been done." What can a stepmother do to help kids who have lost traditions and old routines in their lives? Just as importantly, how can she avoid not making it worse?

If you are a newcomer to the family system, you can make an effort to honour the pre-existing traditions. If you have kids of your own, try to honour the pre-existing traditions you have established with the children, too.

As much as humanly possible, refrain from making abrupt reforms immediately. Observe how things are being done in your spouse's family and try not to disrupt these routines right away.

Early in our marriage, I added in some unique ingredients to the macaroni and cheese dish. It was extra creamy, which I thought the kids would appreciate. It turned out that their dad already had a special "cheesy Mac" recipe, and they preferred his version.

In fact, eating Dad's dish was one of their traditions. Their dad didn't see the significance of this yummy concoction, but to the kids, it was important. Dad made it the "right way." So it often is with traditions in our family. We might not even recognize them as important until they are threatened.

This is just a small example, but it can apply to many areas within your family life. In regards to your stepkids' lives, take time to be an observer for a while and ask questions. Don't try to make too many changes all at once without finding out what the original customs are. For your own children, if applicable, try to maintain some of the routines you had established as a single parent, especially at first.

RECOGNIZE EMERGING ROUTINES

Another way to give the gift of tradition is to recognize the little traditions you're doing together as a new stepfamily. As you grow as a family, new routines will arise naturally. You will start to emerge into certain patterns and do things at certain times. Be glad for these new routines and make a note of them with the kids.

Say things like, "We always have a late dinner on Wednesday, don't we?" or "We always watch a movie on Friday nights!" Acknowledging the patterns forming in your lives together will bring a sense of family.

Early in our dating phase, we used to all walk to Dairy Queen on our weekends together. It was quite the trek, and it involved lots of talking and joking, and of course, some wrestling. (It was three males, after all!) We usually all got those treats with ice cream covered with hot fudge and peanuts.

This wasn't great for my waistline, but it was awesome for bonding. It was fun, and the youngest one usually complained that the walk was too long. We didn't talk about anything serious, but just being together was awesome.

This became a routine for us, one that drew us together. After we got married, we developed some new habits. They weren't big things, but they were things that we did. I encourage you to draw out the small things that you are already doing and acknowledge them as routines. In a stepfamily, be careful not to change things too quickly.

DELIBERATELY DEVELOP NEW ROUTINES

The last way of developing a sense of tradition within a blended family is to deliberately set up new routines. This can be anything from regular meal times to chore duties; the important thing is making the home a more predictable place.

I would suggest making this a gradual process, especially if you have older children. Teens are likely to resist new expectations being put upon them and need extra time to adjust. Everyone benefits, though, with some order to keep life organized.

Stepfamily Foundation head Jeannette Lofas says the following about the importance of structure:

> Structure is love. Chaos and unpredictability create low self-esteem in a child.[3]

In her book, *Stepparenting: Everything You Need to Know to Make it Work,* Lofas offers very useful guidance for setting up rules and structure within the home. She emphasizes that this process should be done together as a couple. If you are looking for help in this area, I strongly recommend her book.

Rituals, routines and traditions help form a sense of community and unity. They can be gifts that make a child feel more secure and protected. We need a balance between honouring traditions from the past and seeking ways to slowly develop fresh traditions for the future.

THE GIFT OF INVOLVEMENT

*T*hrough Angus Jones' volatile divorce, he held onto one positive: even his ex-wife could not deny that he was a fantastic father. He was determined to stick to that commitment, despite any difficulty or inconvenience. The fact that he no longer shared a full-time home with his children did not stop him from being deeply engrossed in his children's activities. Jones explains:

> Every time they did something, we were involved. Whether it was band, baseball or camp, I was helping out with leadership and volunteering. Even their mother acknowledged that I was a good dad.

THE BENEFITS OF INVOLVEMENT

When you and your partner get involved in the activities of

the children, you're going against the norm. Historically, children from stepfamilies have had more social problems, behavioural issues and academic concerns. Studies prove that stepchildren spend less time with their parents than children from intact homes.[1]

The best plan to ensure that your family is an exception to these statistics is to become involved in the kids' activities and interests. This means going out to school activities, performances and sports games.

THE AWKWARDNESS OF INVOLVEMENT

Going to activities can be uncomfortable when there is an uneasy relationship with your stepchild's mother Being present and creating memories are worth paying the price of a few awkward hours here and there.

I will give one caveat here. There may be times where being at events will make it hard on the performers because they feel pressure to make sure everyone gets along. In this case, use your best judgment. There may even be times when staying away is an opportunity to demonstrate love.

THE MESSAGE OF INVOLVEMENT

As a high school English teacher, I taught several burly, rowdy teenage boys whose lives revolved around sports. When I went to my principal for help getting through to these students, he suggested I watch some volleyball games. This administrator was so wise! Seeing these loud "troublemakers" on the courts gave me a whole new appreciation for the young men. In their domain, they demonstrated leadership, consideration and mastery.

Them seeing me in the stands let them know I that cared about them as more than just a "giver of grades." I was interested in what they were interested in. The next day, I could praise them with a good game and genuinely mean it. My relationship with these athletes grew much deeper, and my teaching became more effective, all because of a few hours spent on some bleachers.

When you stand in the bleachers to watch children in your life play or sit in the chair to see them perform, you are sending a powerful message: you are my priority, and I am proud of you!

13

THE GIFT OF THE MUNDANE

I remember one occasion when my husband, stepson and I were waiting for our taxes to be done at the local department store. I shopped for clothes, while the two of them explored the rest of the establishment.

When I came out of the dressing room, I saw two crazy guys heading straight towards me with some weird kitchen gadget. We need this!" my stepson exclaimed. Then father and son proceeded to tell me all the bizarre uses for this ridiculous product, none of which were its intended use. It was hilarious, and I couldn't help but burst into laughter at their silliness.

Little ordinary moments like this are a gift that we often take for granted. I call this the "gift of the mundane." The *Alpha Dictionary* defines *mundane* as "pedestrian, commonplace, trite, ordinary."[1] In other words, this gift is the gift of doing ordinary life together.

It is sharing chores, errands and walks. It is hanging out in a department store while waiting for taxes to get done or setting the table for a bowl of spaghetti. It is sharing the commonplace activities of your life.

When the boys were teenagers, my astute husband consistently created opportunities for me to experience the mundane with the boys. He would drop us off at the grocery store and say, "You guys pick up some food, and I'll be back in half an hour after I get the oil changed. Instinctively, he understood the need for us to spend time together, in order to bond, and took action to make it happen.

Look for opportunities to do everyday activities with your stepchild. Take a walk to the store together. Do the dishes. Watch a television show together. Offer to play a video game.

Whatever it is, the key is that you're *doing* something together. A shared activity takes your mind off the awkwardness of not knowing each other, freeing you to enjoy each other's company without the pressure.

"Doing life together" is a fantastic opportunity to bond by sharing a task. You both have a common goal, which can help bring you together. It can also be a chance to have a non-threatening conversation. Shopping together is an awesome time to chat about favourite foods. A few minutes spent sorting laundry can be a chance to talk about what is happening at school. Casual, quick interactions are a critical part of building your relationship over time.

Sometimes subjects will arise naturally out of the activity you are participating in. Just keep things light and try to keep the conversation going. Ask simple questions that are not threatening. Share what's going on in your world without "oversharing."

These wise words from Robert Brault sum it up very nicely:

> Enjoy the little things, for one day, you may look back and realize they were the big things.[2]

Appreciating the mundane might sound boring but these little moments form the fabric of our lives.

14

THE GIFT OF FUN

*T*he 1980's song by Cyndi Lauper was called "Girls Just Wanna Have Fun"[1] and we could easily change it to say, "kids just wanna have fun!" Even the most seemingly serious child will let go and be goofy if they feel safe enough.

The next gift we will examine is called the "gift of fun." One of the most powerful ways that a human being begins to feel close to someone is to have fun with them. Laughter is good medicine, indeed: for rejection, sadness, and anger.

The more pleasant memories you can share, the more you can build your relationship on neutral ground. One of the ways that kids grow to know you is when they have fun with you.

As adult women, we are all busy and have so many responsibilities. Even though we acknowledge, in theory, that it's important to have fun, let's be honest, finding the time is tricky. Therefore, I suggest that you schedule some fun time into your calendar. If you don't, it might not actually happen!

Of course, like the weird gadget in the department store, fun is not always planned, but sometimes planning goes a long way, too. Here are some tips for planning some fun activities:

1. *Plan a light-hearted activity that everyone in the family can enjoy. You don't have to spend money to do this! There are many things you can easily do for free.*
2. *Do something appropriate for the ages and skill levels of all the children.*
3. *Don't try to teach any lessons or force conversation. Keep it light!*
4. *Turn off your cell phone and be present. Encourage everyone else to stay off their device, too!*
5. *If the stepchildren are not very open to you yet, you may wish to let the suggestion for the activity come from their father.*

Remember, the primary goal is that some laughter will result! Don't worry too much about making everything perfect – just have fun! When you are able to let go and have a good time, the children can see another side of you that they may not experience every day. Kids are not the only ones to benefit from some fun activities — we need it, too!

To help you out, I have included a list of ideas. These are just to get you started. If you would like a copy of these ideas, sign up here:

https://secondmarriage.xyz/24-fun-ideas-to-do-with-kids-45444/

TWENTY-EIGHT FUN IDEAS

Out of the House Ideas

1. Go to an indoor archery range. Everyone can play, and they let you pop balloons!
2. Check out the local fair for games, rides and fattening junk food!
3. Go to a local festival, whether a winter carnival in January or an outdoor music concert in July.
4. Go swimming at your local beach or swimming pool.
5. Try out the local trampoline facility, where kids can jump to their heart's content.
6. Get some bowling done. It's very low stress!
7. Go for a picnic or a barbeque at the park (or your backyard) and bring Frisbees and balls.
8. Go for a walk to your nearest ice cream shop. Take time discussing the weird flavours available and why you all prefer certain flavours over others.
9. Check out your city's planetarium or museum. Make a quest to check out all your community's museums within the next six months.
10. Take a road trip to a town or city that is an hour away and have dinner there together.
11. Go to an amusement park, indoor or outdoor, depending on the weather.
12. Take them to the airport to watch the planes take off, and then go for ice cream.

13. Go for a photography walk where you all take pictures of your surroundings together, using your phones. Then compare your pics!

14. Go for a walk or a bike ride together.

In the House Ideas

1. View a movie together. The key is to get one that incorporates elements that all of you can enjoy. Popcorn is a bonus!

2. Play video games together. This is an excellent way to get into their world, and don't worry: they will be happy to show you how.

3. Get into some old-fashioned board or card games. These are great for getting to know each other!

4. Make pizzas or (tacos) together.

5. Tackle some crafts as a family.

6. Play icebreaker games such as "This or That?" or "Twenty Questions."

7. Follow a television series together that you can all get into. Reality TV shows such as *Master Chef* can be fun because there's lots of room for discussion and cheering.

8. Clean the house together but make challenges such as "pick up 30 things" and maybe small prizes for winners.

9. Have a scavenger or treasure hunt. This is a lot of work to set up, but it's a blast!

10. For younger kids, get down on the floor and play with their toys with them.

11. For younger kids, play pretend. Don't worry – they will show you how!
12. If you have a pet, spend time together playing with the dog or the cat.
13. Read a book aloud for everyone to hear. If you are a family of faith, read the Scriptures and pray together.
14. Put on a play together! If they tend towards the dramatic side, let them plan it. If not, you lead it.

15

THE GIFT OF DISCRETION

*B*efore you married your spouse, you likely did not realize how inextricably linked you would become with your spouse's ex-partner. Even if the mother has passed away, the children will always have a bond with her. How we handle this relationship will have a profound impact on the child's well-being.

One of the key determining factors of how well children fare in a breakup is how the adults handle conflict.[1] Exposing children to conflict puts them in the agonizing position of being "in the middle."

Because our husband's ex-partner is the children's mother, we must always remember to respect her role in their lives, no matter how difficult. It is crucial to remember that a person's mother is usually the most influential and beloved person in his life. Therefore, we must never say anything negative about a child's biological mother to him.

When a child hears his parent being disparaged, it makes him feel as if he himself is being criticized because he is part of his parent. Think of a child on the playground. He will fight and bicker with his brother every evening, but if another kid badmouths him, then the war is on! We all instinctively want to protect our own flesh and blood.

When we act maturely and are careful with our tongues, it is called "discretion," which is also a great gift that you can give to your stepchild.

Discretion is an old-fashioned word that means "the quality of having good judgment, or cautious reserve in speech."[2] One anonymous writer defined discretion as "not always saying everything that is on your mind." The writer continued by saying: "Just because something's true, it doesn't mean you have to say it."

YOUR SPOUSE'S DISCRETION

As a stepmom, you hold considerable influence over how your husband talks about the child's mother. Being disciplined in this area is perhaps harder for him especially if he is still hurting from a divorce.

But he will only serve to alienate his children further if he spouts off about how much he dislikes their mother. Encourage him to hold back negative talk in front of the children, for their sake. By doing this, he is demonstrating to the children that they are not required to choose between their mom and dad. Loving both of them is okay!

Your influence in this area is vital. A recent report from Justice Canada stated that:

> Children whose parents remain hostile and aggressive, locked in ongoing high conflict are more apt to have behavioural problems, emotional difficulties and social difficulties (Johnston 1994). They are also more likely to lack self-esteem (Kelly 1993).[3]

In other words, kids do worse in almost every way, when their parents are fighting. Try to hold onto that truth, no matter how extreme your situation.

We are like diplomats, who must practice complete discretion in their profession. They are required to maintain the face of respect and composure, no matter their true feelings.

One anonymous writer defined *diplomacy* in this manner:

> Diplomacy: the business of handling a porcupine without disturbing the quills.

REASONS FOR STEPMOM-BIO-MOM CONFLICT

Why is there so much potential conflict between the stepmom and the biological mother? Jenna Korf, from the blog *Stepmother Help*, helps us understand the dynamic in her article titled "Why does my husband's ex-wife hate me?"[4]

This article can be found here:

http://www.stepmomhelp.com/stepfamily-q-a-why-does-my-husbands-ex-wife-hate-me

In this powerful piece, Korf points out how the biological

mom is put in a situation where she is sharing parenting tasks with a stranger. A strange woman is now seeing and spending time with her child on a regular basis, and she has no idea if she is trustworthy or not.

Finally, the stepmother can be a constant reminder that she and her ex-partner were not able to make it and that he has moved on. No matter how uncomfortable it is to consider the viewpoint of the bio-mom, it is good to know where the conflict might be coming from.

In conclusion, the gift of discretion makes the wise, adult choice not to let grown-up conflicts trickle down to the children.

THE GIFT OF AUTHENTICITY

One of the things I love about animals is that they are always 100 percent themselves. When my cat, Gray Eyes, is mad about something, there is no confusion. She meows at me incessantly until I pay attention to her and figure out what is bothering her.

When my Great Pyrenees adolescent dog, Snowball, is happy, her tail wags so hard it knocks down a few papers that might be in her way. We never wonder what she is feeling because her whole body radiates her emotions.

We can always count on our pets to be genuine and show their true selves to us, but with people, it's not quite so simple. We spend a lot of our time wondering who we can trust and who might be hiding their true intentions.

As stepmothers, feeling like we can be ourselves is a crucial concern for us. We are in a situation where it is difficult to be genuine because the relationships and dynamics are so complicated.

We have to be careful to avoid hurt feelings and misunderstandings. We may be perturbed with something our spouse is doing but we try to wait for the right way and right time to bring it up. We may struggle with trying to communicate our feelings to our stepchildren without offending them or pushing them further away.

We may find our relationship with our partner's ex to be difficult and full of conflict, but we know that is not something we can talk about in front of the children, so we hold things in. We try to keep the peace in that relationship, so things are easier on the children.

NOT THEIR REAL MOTHER

With the complex dynamics, it is no surprise that we struggle to be authentic in this relationship at times. In fact, the British version of the Cambridge dictionary defines a "stepmother" as "the woman who is married to someone's father but who is not their *real* mother"[1] (emphasis mine).

When the very definition of our role contains the words, "not real," it is no wonder that we contend with insecurity sometimes. The dictionary defines *authenticity* as "the quality of being real or true."[2] It is often used when referring to a painting or an artifact, as in "the experts weren't sure if that copy of the manuscript was authentic or a fake."

FOUR TIPS FOR AUTHENTICITY

How do we maintain our authenticity in a situation that implies that we are "not real"? Here are four ways that we can stay ourselves within the complexity of a stepfamily.

I. **Remember Your Passion.** Two years into our marriage, the stress was at a climax. We were all still adjusting to one another, my job was very pressured, and our relationship was in trouble. It felt like I couldn't take anything else on. Somehow, I found a couple of hours every Saturday to create art collages on a site called Polyvore.

The reaction from my husband was less than encouraging. He wondered how I could sit on a computer when there was obviously so much to do! As he sailed by me, fixing something or roughhousing with his boys, I sat at my desk located in our busy, chaotic living room and created. I lost myself for a couple of delightful hours in the wonder of my imagination. My soul soaked it up, and it helped me survive!

If you have lost yourself along the way, I have four questions for you:

- What is your passion?
- What one thing makes you feel most alive?
- What did you yearn to do before life got crazy?
- Are you still doing it?

If not, please find some time for your passions, even if only an hour or two a week! Find a way to do something that reminds you of *you* – beyond being a wife, a stepmom, an employee and a cleaner.

2. **Care for yourself.** Concentrate on making healthier choices for your own body, even if your family doesn't practice these same habits. I think we all know self-care is important, but it is difficult to allow ourselves the time.

Becoming a stepmother means that we adjust our former lifestyle to the needs and preferences of our new family. Our schedules change. Our responsibilities change. This can also mean that some healthy habits may fall away.

Stress also makes it difficult to maintain the discipline of careful choices. Making just one small change in your day can make a significant difference. Try to do just one thing that will make you feel healthier, whether it's eating more vegetables or getting more sleep. Don't attempt to do everything all at once. One small change is much more attainable.

3. **Be vulnerable sometimes.** In the nighttime drama *Nashville*[3] the beloved character, Raina James, dies in a terrible car accident. Her husband is utterly distraught for over a year but finally takes the step of starting to date again. His youngest daughter, Daphne, outright ignores her father's friend and talks in a curt tone that demonstrates her quiet disapproval.

After a few weeks of this behaviour, the new lady in her father's life asks to speak with Daphne alone. Sitting in the girl's bedroom, Jesse shares that she is scared, too, and reassures the teenager that she has absolutely no illusion about replacing Daphne's mom. Instead, she asks to be her friend. Daphne agrees and the two hug.

What hit me about this exchange is how much Daphne and Jesse had in common. They both loved the same man. They both felt awkward and nervous about the situation. A willingness to share her feelings sincerely worked in this possible future stepmom's favour.

Her vulnerability opened the way for this confused, hurting teenage girl to be vulnerable in return, and was instrumental in finally breaking the barrier between these two females in Deacon's life.

Try to be honest about what you want from the relationship and how you wish things could get better. Letting someone in and sharing your heart can sometimes work far better than a "top-down approach" where you demand results without explaining the reason why.

Sometimes the most effective way for a child to open up is to share honestly with them. By sharing your feelings, you are letting them know you are vulnerable and that they can hurt you with their actions. I would not recommend doing this all the time, but once in a while, it can be an effective strategy for connection.

4. **Let others in.** Before I wrote my book about second marriages, I thought I knew no one who was remarried. When my book was published, I was quite shocked that many people came forward and shared that either they themselves were in a second marriage, or their daughter or son, or close friend was.

Before I wrote the book, I *thought* I was alone, but in reality, I was not. As stepmothers, we may feel very isolated. Our problems seem different and strange compared to the biological parents that we know. It is difficult to explain what we are going through.

Therefore, we may isolate ourselves out of embarrassment and shame. When you're feeling this way, know that you really are *not* alone! Take a chance and share a bit about your situation with a friend or family member. You may find that they relate because of something going on in their own life.

Another way to reach out is to find a support group specifically for stepmoms. There are many Facebook groups that focus on this part of life. You might also find something in your area. If you're the organizing type, you may even consider starting one yourself!

Lastly, if you have cut yourself from family and friends because of the stress in your life, let them back in! Go out with friends and family that know you as more than a stepmom. Have some fun and forget about that part of your life for a few hours. You were a woman, a friend, a sister, maybe a mother, before you became a stepmom. This role does not define you. When you are yourself, you are also bringing your "true self" to all the relationships in your blended family.

THE GIFT OF STABILITY

*B*efore my husband and I got married, I asked Vern's youngest son for permission to marry his father. This twelve-year-old boy told me, "I am the kind of person who thinks people should be able to marry whoever makes them happy. So, as long as you make my dad happy, I don't mind."

I doubt that he remembers that conversation today, ten years later, but there is more wisdom than he was even aware of in that exchange. He said that he wanted his father to be happy, and isn't that what every child wants?

As much as children do want their parents to be happy deep inside, they may feel competitive with their stepmother and desire her gone. What they don't realize, however, is that getting rid of the stepmom will not solve their problems but will only create another loss in their lives.

Ron Deal, the author of many books on the stepfamily, explains the need for a secure relationship this way:

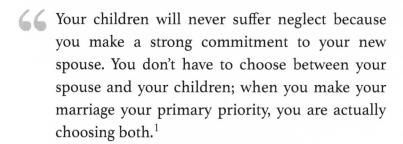 Your children will never suffer neglect because you make a strong commitment to your new spouse. You don't have to choose between your spouse and your children; when you make your marriage your primary priority, you are actually choosing both.[1]

Deal makes the salient point that your children will not suffer when you prioritize your spouse! No, a healthy marriage means that the kids will grow up in a healthy environment. On the other hand, if the adults are in constant conflict, the children will be adversely affected.

One of the finest gifts that you can give your stepchild is the gift of a stable relationship. The child has already been through the life-altering upheaval of either divorce or bereavement. If you and her father were to break up, this would mean *another* crisis: another change over which she has no control.

Another benefit of making your marriage work is that by doing so, you may influence the child to have some faith in marriage itself, demonstrating by your example that some relationships do last.

TIPS FOR STABILITY

Even if we agree that a strong relationship is of benefit to all involved, we may not know how to attain this goal. How do we navigate the complications of a second marriage, and strengthen that relationship? My husband and I struggled greatly, and at times, talked about divorce. Our challenges led me to want to help others in a similar situation, and led me to writing my first book.

Here are four tips for a stronger bond between you and your partner.

1. **Acknowledge the complications.** First of all, it is important to recognize the complications you are dealing with, complexities that those in first marriages don't have. You are likely dealing with former partner problems, financial stress, and stepfamily adjustments.

Don't expect things to be as simple as an original marriage and acknowledge that you may need extra time to process and handle the extra issues that come up.

2. **Find alone time.** Next, as a couple, you will probably have to fight for time alone together. Make the most of those rare moments of quiet. Unlike other newlyweds without children, you will not have that idyllic "honeymoon period" where the two of you are alone for at least a year.

On my website, I've created a fun resource called *11 Ideas for Connecting with your Spouse, when you don't have any time.* You will receive some creative ideas for quick bonding activities as a couple.You can get this mini-book at the address below.

https://secondmarriage.xyz/connection-ideas/

3. **Find common interests.** In a stepfamily marriage, there are many things that can potentially divide us. The biological

parent and stepparent are often on opposites of an issue because of the very nature of stepfamilies. We are constantly adjusting to the kids being with us, and then being at the other home.

Therefore, finding common interests and goals is especially important for the couple who have so many potential dividers. Seek to find a common project that you can do together. For my husband and me, it was our pets.

Remember the commonalities, whatever they are, that drew you together as a couple. Whether it's music or movies, seek for similar interests and pursue them together.

4. **Get Outside help.** Finally, don't be afraid to seek outside help if you need it. There is nothing shameful about needing someone to help you sort the complex issues that arise when merging two families together. Marriage is challenging, and a professional can help you navigate the tricky waters.

For my husband and me, a counsellor was the only one who got through to us and helped us save our marriage. Consider a marriage counsellor or a marriage coach. Books can also be very helpful and encouraging for giving ideas. There are a plethora of resources out there. Check the end of this book for a link to resources that I recommend.

In conclusion, stability is a gift that takes hard work and commitment, but it will benefit all members of your family.

18

THE GIFT OF ENDURANCE

*A*ngus and Betty Jones have been married for over 25 years. Their first few years of marriage were tumultuous, and the threat of divorce constantly hung over their head. Angus's boys, especially the oldest, did not accept their new stepmom.

In the beginning, the couple fought a lot but eventually learned to get along. Both of them took mediation courses at their jobs, which helped them learn to negotiate. The arguing gradually calmed down.

Last Christmas, the two of them flew to England to visit their youngest boy and his kids. The grandchildren love their Grandma Betty and can't wait to see her. In the summer, they come to stay with them and enjoy looking at the special fairy garden reserved just for her granddaughters.

Betty and Angus are both set to retire next year and are

looking forward to travelling and pursuing their interests. Is their marriage perfect? No, but they have been building a life together for over a quarter of a century.

It was tempting to quit when they were struggling so much, but they persevered. When you meet them, it is easy to observe the teasing banter, the quiet respect and sense of teamwork.

Betty never did get too close with the oldest boy. He still keeps his distance, but she has endured. They are now proud grandparents. Neither one of them gave up.

The *Merriam-Webster Dictionary Online* defines endurance as "the ability to withstand hardship or adversity; especially: the ability to sustain a prolonged stressful effort or activity."[1] We often think of endurance in terms of running a marathon. The runner does not stop until she has finished the race.

Isn't that what stepparenting is about? Holding on for the long haul? We keep going, and we don't walk away from the relationship with our partner or the children. And yes, there are hardships and adversity, and prolonged stressful efforts and activity!

For my last book, *Second Marriage: An Insider's Guide to Hope, Healing & Love,* I conducted several interviews. At the end, I asked these remarried individuals for some parting advice to other remarried couples. Every single one had some variation of this encouraging message to offer. They said: "Don't give up! It gets easier!" All of them had gone through devastating times but were grateful that they had not given up.

When my husband and I first got married, I came across an

excellent book on marriage called *The Smart Stepfamily*,[2] by Ron Deal. In the volume, he says that it takes, on average, seven years for stepfamilies to come together. When I read that statistic, I recoiled in horror! Seven years? I thought, by that time, the boys will be out of the house and in university!

Although I felt like throwing the book across the room in disgust the first time I saw this prediction, it was actually quite accurate. Stepfamilies take a long time to come together. Every situation is different – there are many factors to consider. Not everyone will take that long – this is only a rough average. Regardless of the exact time it takes for things to start to feel more normal, endurance is critical.

YOU ARE BUILDING A LEGACY

*D*on't you love Christmas shopping? There's something so exciting about seeing all the people in the mall, each with the same goal in mind: presents! I've always loved Christmas shopping, but I especially enjoyed shopping for my mom because she showed so much appreciation for the presents we gave her.

When I was ten years old, I bought her a seashell jewelry box that she kept on her dresser for years. A decade later, I gave her a soapstone sculpture of a young boy with his dog, and she proudly displayed it on her living room coffee table for as long as I can remember.

Sixteen years ago, our family was looking forward to Christmas because it was our first holiday with a new baby in the family: my mom's first grandchild. As we all doted over this precious infant, there was a sense of sadness in the air. My mother had been fighting a rare form of breast cancer for almost five years. We were all praying for her healing, but the pain was becoming unbearable for her, and her body seemed to be falling apart.

I knew this might be her last season with us, and I felt determined to spoil her the best I could. My budget was limited, but I was able to get a staff discount at the Christian organization where I worked and picked up two gorgeous snow globes, along with some other pretty trinkets.

My goal was to make it as special as possible for her, knowing she might not have much more time with us. Less than three months later, on March 14, 2002, my sweet mama left this earth.

The trinkets I presented my mother on that Christmas Eve were beautiful, and she expressed her appreciation, as always. They were utterly worthless, though, in comparison to the immeasurable gifts she bestowed upon me her entire life: her unshaken confidence in my abilities, her time, her kindness, her counsel. My mom gave of herself in any way she could to make my sister and me succeed.

Maybe reading about my mom reminds you of the gifts that your mother, father or grandparents gave you. They gave you their time, their energy, their love. The endowments a parent bestows upon a child last a lifetime and live on even after they are gone. These are the presents one never regrets giving! These are the favours that form a family and eventually, shape a legacy.

As a stepmom, you are influencing a family, too, but *your* family is radically different than the one that you imagined.

You are helping to raise children that aren't all yours. You may be blending two sets of siblings together.

Whether the kids in your life appreciate you right now is not the point. *Your contributions are of great significance.* You are building a legacy. Never underestimate your impact.

THANK YOU

 Hi there! I just wanted to thank you so much for picking up this book and reading. I hope you found it beneficial and encouraging. If you would like to pass on the love, I would so much appreciate you leaving a review for me. I read all the reviews and am always thrilled to receive a new one. Thank you in advance!

Also, if you are interested in hearing from me on a regular basis, you can sign up for my mailing list here:

https://secondmarriage.xyz/get-updates-from-sharilee-swaity3445/

RECOMMENDED RESOURCES

For a list of recommended resources on stepfamilies and remarriage, please go to the following page:

https://secondmarriage.xyz/recommended-resources8587/

Second Marriage: An Insider's Guide to Hope, Healing & Love

(Available in Ebook, Paperback and Audiobook versions.)

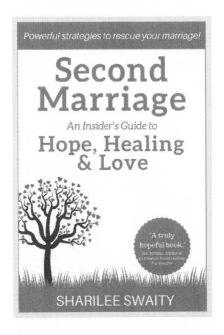

ABOUT THE AUTHOR

Sharilee Swaity helps give couples hope for their marriages. She has been a stepmom for ten years. She and her husband, Vern, live in the woods of Northern Manitoba with their two cats and Great Pyrenees dog named Snowball. Sharilee has been writing about relationships for nine years. She has a Bachelor of Education and over ten years of classroom experience. You can find her relationship blog at http://secondmarriage.xyz.

f facebook.com/secondmarriagetransformed

twitter.com/secondmarriageɪ

instagram.com/lifeinwoods

g goodreads.com/Sharilee_Swaity

NOTES

INTRODUCTION

1. Ron Deal, "Marriage, Family, & Stepfamily Statistics," *Smart Stepfamilies*, last modified April 2019, https://www.smartstepfamilies.com/view/statistics (accessed October 31, 2019).
2. Jeannette Lofas, *Stepparenting: Everything You Need to Know to Make it Work* (New York: Citadel Press Books, 2004).
3. *Secret Millionaire*, ABC.

2. THE STEPCHILD'S LOSS

1. *The Crown*, "Hyde Park Corner" Season 1, Episode 3, written by Peter Morgan, Netflix, November 4, 2016.
2. Bella DePaulo, "What Is the Divorce Rate, Really?" *Psychology Today*, February 2, 2017, https://www.psychologytoday.com/us/blog/living-single/201702/what-is-the-divorce-rate-really.
3. Deal, "Marriage, Family, & Stepfamily Statistics."
4. Jane Anderson, "The impact of family structure on the health of children: Effects of divorce," *The Linacre Quarterly*, November, 2014; 81(4): 378–387, https://www.ncbi.nlm.nih.gov/pmc/articles/PMC4240051/#
5. Pauline O'Conner, Ottawa: Department of Justice, 2004, "Voice and Support: Programs for Children Experiencing Parental Separation and Divorce," http://www.justice.gc.ca/eng/rp-pr/fl-lf/divorce/2004_2/p2.html.
6. Anderson, "The impact of family structure on the health of children: Effects of divorce."
7. Victoria H. Raveis, Karolynn Siegel, Daniel Karus, "Children's Psychological Distress Following the Death of a Parent" *Journal of Youth and Adolescence*, (1999) 28: 165. https://link.springer.com/article/10.1023/A:1021697230387.
8. Raveis, "Children's Psychological Distress Following the Death of a Parent."
9. *The Parent Trap*, *1961*, directed by David Smith, Burbank, California: Walt Disney Pictures.

10. Conner, *Voice and Support: Programs for Children Experiencing Parental Separation and Divorce.*

3. THE GIFT OF COMPASSION

1. "Humboldt Broncos bus crash: What we know so far," *Globe and Mail*, last modified April 11, 2018, https://www.theglobeandmail.com/canada/article-humboldt-broncos-hockey-bus-crash-saskatchewan-explainer/ (Accessed October 1, 2018).
2. Joe Eskenazi, *The Jewish News of Northern Carolina,* December 22, 2000, https://www.jweekly.com/2000/12/22/effects-of-divorce-last-well-into-adulthood-expert-says/, (Accessed December 15, 2019).

4. THE GIFT OF ACCEPTANCE

1. Ted Widmer 2011, "Lincoln's Other Mother," *The New York Times*, January 29, 2011, https://opinionator.blogs.nytimes.com/2011/01/29/lincolns-other-mother/ (Accessed October 2018).
2. Gillian Brockell, "Abraham Lincoln's 'angel mother' and the second 'mama' who outlived him," *Washington Post,* May 12, 2018, https://www.washingtonpost.com/news/retropolis/wp/2018/05/12/abraham-lincolns-angel-mother-and-the-mama-who-outlived-him (Accessed October 2018).
3. Widmer, "Lincoln's Other Mother."
4. Burlingame, Michael. *The Inner World of Abraham Lincoln* (Champaign: University of Illinois Press, 1997) 38.
5. Ibid, 137.
6. Lowell H. Harrison, *Lincoln of Kentucky,* (Lexington: The University Press of Kentucky, 2009), 30.
7. Widmer, "Lincoln's Other Mother."
8. Ibid.
9. Paul Tournier Quotes, *BrainyMedia Inc*, 2020, https://www.brainyquote.com/quotes/paul_tournier_119360, accessed January 7, 2020.
10. Thomas Gordon*, Parent Effectiveness Training Book* (New York City: Harmony 2000), 38.
11. Patricia Papernow, *Becoming a Stepfamily: Patterns of Development in Remarried Families,* (Hillsdale, N.J.: The Analytic Press, 1993).
12. Sharilee Swaity. "Personality differences in the stepfamily." *Stepmom Help.* September 13, 2017, https://www.stepmomhelp.com/guest-post-by-sharilee-swaity-personality-differences-in-the-stepfamily/.

5. THE GIFT OF PATIENCE

1. Patricia Papernow, *Surviving and Thriving in a Stepfamily Relationship* (Oxfordshire: Routledge 2013), 27.

6. THE GIFT OF FORGIVENESS

1. *Your Dictionary Online.* s.v. forgive, accessed December 16, 2019. https://www.yourdictionary.com/forgive.

7. THE GIFT OF ENCOURAGEMENT

1. *Oxford Dictionary*, s.v. encouragement, accessed Nov. 16, 2019, https://www.lexico.com/en/definition/encouragement.
2. *Cambridge Dictionary Online,* s.v. encouragement, accessed Sept 29, 2019, https://dictionary.cambridge.org/dictionary/english/encouragement.

8. THE GIFT OF LISTENING

1. Suzy Yehl Marta, *Healing the Hurt, Restoring the Hope.* (Toronto, Ontario: Rodale Books 2003), 179.
2. Raveis, "Children's Psychological Distress Following the Death of a Parent."
3. O'Conner, Department of Justice Canada, *Voice and Support: Programs for Children Experiencing Parental Separation and Divorce.*
4. Ibid.
5. Paul Tournier, *To Understand Each Other* (Westminster: John Knox Press 1967), 25.

10. THE GIFT OF DADDY TIME

1. United States Census Bureau, *Custodial Mothers and Fathers and Their Child Support: 2013,* by Timothy Grill, Report Number P60-255. https://www.census.gov/content/dam/Census/library/publications/2016/demo/P60-255.pdf (accessed Sept 29th 2019).

11. THE GIFT OF TRADITION

1. Sister Mary Agnes Dombroski, "The Power to Heal," filmed in Piscataqua River, Tedx Talks, 15:25. https://www.youtube.com/watch?v=beNIT5qXxvo
2. American Psychological Association, *Children and Trauma: Update for Mental Health Professionals*, https://www.apa.org/pi/families/resources/children-trauma-update (Washington, D.C.: 2008) (Accessed Nov. 25, 2019)
3. Lofas, *Stepparenting: Everything you need to Know to Make it Work*, 23.

12. THE GIFT OF INVOLVEMENT

1. Marilyn Coleman, Lawrence Ganong, and Mark Fine, "Reinvestigating Remarriage: Another Decade of Progress," *Journal of Marriage and Family* (2000) 62(4), pg. 1288-1307, https://libres.uncg.edu/ir/uncg/f/M_Fine_Reinvestigating_2000.pdf (Accessed February 14, 2018).

13. THE GIFT OF THE MUNDANE

1. *Alpha Dictionary Online*, s.v. mundane, accessed September 29, 2019, https://www.alphadictionary.com/goodword/word/mundane.
2. Robert Brault, *Round up the Usual Subjects: Thoughts on Just About Everything*, (Createspace 2014).

14. THE GIFT OF FUN

1. Cindy Lauper, vocal performance of "Girls Just Wanna Have Fun," by Robert Hazard, recorded June 1983, Record Plant, New York City, New York.

15. THE GIFT OF DISCRETION

1. JoAnne Pedro-Carroll, PhD, "How Parents Can Help Children Cope With Separation/Divorce," *Encyclopedia on Early Childhood Development*, ed. Robert E. Emery, last modified November 2011, http://www.child-encyclopedia.com/divorce-and-separation/according-experts/how-

parents-can-help-children-cope-separationdivorce, (Accessed November 18, 2019).

2. *Meriam-Webster Dictionary Online.* v.s. discretion, accessed Nov. 17, 2019. https://www.merriam-webster.com/dictionary/discretion.

3. O'Conner, *Voice and Support: Programs for Children Experiencing Parental Separation and Divorce.*

4. Jenna Korf, "Why Does My Husband's Ex-Wife Hate Me?" *Stepmom Help,* October 11, 2012, https://www.stepmomhelp.com/stepfamily-q-a-why-does-my-husbands-ex-wife-hate-me.

16. THE GIFT OF AUTHENTICITY

1. *Cambridge Dictionary Online,* s.v. "stepmother," accessed November 17, 2019, https://dictionary.cambridge.org/dictionary/english/stepmother.

2. Ibid, s.v. "authenticity," accessed November 17, 2019.

3. *Nashville,* Season 6, Episode 6. "Beneath Still Waters," directed by Dan Lerner, aired February 8, 2018 on CMT.

17. THE GIFT OF STABILITY

1. Ron Deal, "Placing Your Spouse in the Front Seat of Your Heart." *Family Life,* http://www.familylife.com/articles/topics/blended-family/remarriage/staying-married/placing-your-spouse-in-the-front-seat-of-your-heart, accessed February 22, 2018.

18. THE GIFT OF ENDURANCE

1. *Merriam-Webster Dictionary.* s.v. "endurance," accessed Nov. 17, 2019, https://www.merriam-webster.com/dictionary/endurance.

2. Ron Deal, *The Smart Stepfamily: Seven Steps to a Healthy Family* (Ada Michigan: Bethany House Publishers 2014), 40.

Made in the USA
Middletown, DE
20 January 2021